MASON JAR

CRAFTS

for Kids

MASON JAR CRAFTS for Kids

More Than 25 Cool, Crafty Projects to Make
for Your Friends, Your Family,
and Yourself!

LINDA Z. BRADEN

Sky Pony Press
New York

Sky Pony Press books may be purchased in bulk at special discounts for sales promotion, corporate gifts, fund-raising, or educational purposes. Special editions can also be created to specifications. For details, contact the Special Sales Department, Sky Pony Press, 307 West 36th Street, 11th Floor, New York, NY 10018 or info@ skyhorsepublishing.com.

Sky Pony® is a registered trademark of Skyhorse Publishing, Inc.®, a Delaware corporation.

Visit our website at www.skyponypress.com.

10 9 8 7 6 5 4 3 2

Manufactured in China, December 2014
This product conforms to CPSIA 2008

Library of Congress Cataloging-in-Publication Data

Braden, Linda Z.
Mason jar crafts for kids : more than 25 cool, crafty projects to make for your friends, your family, and yourself! / Linda Z. Braden.
pages cm
Summary: "Accompanied by photo tutorials and helpful step-by-step instructions, these projects are kid-friendly and offer a variety of options for both beginning and more advanced DIY fans. Be inspired and discover the endless possibilities with the world's most famous jar!"-- Provided by publisher.
Audience: 7+.
Audience: Grades 4 to 6.
Includes index.
ISBN 978-1-63220-413-4 (pb : alk. paper)
1. Storage jars—Juvenile literature. 2. Handicraft—Juvenile literature. 3. Glass painting and staining—Juvenile literature. 4. Decoration and ornament—Juvenile literature. I. Title.
TT157.B727 2015
745.5—dc23
2014040035

Cover and interior design by Erin Seaward-Hiatt
Cover photo credit Linda Z. Braden

Ebook ISBN: 978-1-63220-830-9

CONTENTS

Sharing the Mason Jar Love: Gift Ideas

Mad Science with Mason Jars: Jarring Science Experiments

Introduction

Welcome to *Mason Jar Crafts for Kids!* This is a book written just for you—*kids!*—and filled with fun, creative, and unconventional craft ideas using Mason jars.

Now crafting is not the first thing that comes to mind when most people think of Mason jars. No, most would think of canning and preserving foods. That's because Mason jars were originally created to preserve fresh fruits and vegetables. Most likely, that's how your mother or your grandmother or your great-great-grandmother used Mason jars.

But that was then, and this is now. And Mason jars aren't just for canning anymore. They have emerged from behind closed pantry doors and basement shelves with a new identify—and a new purpose. Plentiful and affordable, Mason jars have been popping up in craft rooms where they are being painted and primped for a repurposed life as vases and drinking glasses and gifts and storage containers. In fact, the ideas for crafting with Mason jars are only limited to your imagination!

A WALK DOWN MASON JAR MEMORY LANE . . .

The Mason jar's long history can be dated back to Napoleon Bonaparte. Turns out the infamous nineteenth-century French emperor and European conqueror had more than battle plans on his mind. He was also concerned about feeding his troops. He offered 12,000 francs—which translates to close to $13,500 in US dollars today—to anyone who could come up with a new way to preserve food.

In 1810, a confectioner named Nicolas Appert rose to the challenge and created the earliest Mason jar predecessor. His revolutionary system involved heating and cooling foods in a glass jar, and then sealing it with a messy wax and wire lid.

Then, in 1812, Thomas Kensett created the first airtight seal. He first used this method on glass jars, but then moved on to tin because, at that time, it was more affordable.

But the true birth of the official Mason jar came in 1858. That's when John Mason patented his unique canning jar design that used a glass jar and a threaded jar lid and cap that formed a tight seal. The greatest innovation was that the parts were reusable, making the Mason jar not only functional, but also affordable. A decade later, Mason further improved his design with a removable rubber ring to create a more effective seal.

When Mason's patent expired in 1879, a number of new players entered the Mason jar arena, including the Ball and Kerr brands that continue to be popular today. Each manufacturer made adjustments and improvements to the original design, but the most notable came in 1915, when Alexander H. Kerr introduced a two-part lid.

By separating the metal lid and the screw band, Kerr helped to improve the seal by preventing bacteria and moisture from spoiling the jar's contents. Close to one hundred years later, this same basic lid design is still in use today.

HOW OLD IS THAT MASON JAR?

After the introduction of home refrigerators in the 1950s, canning and Mason jars fell out of fashion. Until recently, that is. Today, there is a new resurgence in all things Mason jars—from crafting to canning to collecting. In fact, collectors are visiting yard sales and

METAL SCREW BAND

JAR WITH THREADED LIP

METAL LID WITH SEALING COMPOUND

thrift markets looking for as many sizes and as many colors of Mason jars that they can find. Some of the oldest and most rare ones have sold for hundreds of dollars.

Regardless of the age of your jar, the original and iconic pint-size Ball Mason jar shape has remained virtually unchanged. Over the years, though, newer sizes and shapes have been introduced to address the needs of those who use mason jars to preserve fresh produce.

Mason Jar Styles, Sizes & Suggested Canning Uses

JAR	SIZE & STYLE	SUGGESTED USES FOR PRESERVING, SERVING & RECIPES
	Quart size/32 oz regular mouth	Sauces, salsas, syrups, fruits, and vegetables
	Quart size/32 oz wide mouth	Whole fruits and vegetables such as peaches and green beans; ideal for making pickles
	1 ½ pint size/24 oz wide mouth	Longer vegetables like asparagus, cucumbers, and green beans as well as soups and stews

JAR	SIZE & STYLE	SUGGESTED USES FOR PRESERVING, SERVING & RECIPES
	Pint size/16 oz regular mouth	Salsas, sauces, relishes, and pie fillings
	Pint size/16 oz wide mouth	Salsas, sauces, relishes, and fruit butters
	Mug, pint size/16 oz	Serving assorted drink and smoothie recipes
	Elite Collection, pint size/16 oz wide mouth	Fruit dressings, vegetable and fruit salsas, pie fillings, and fruit syrups; elegant enough to take directly from kitchen to table
	Half pint/8 oz regular mouth	Jams, jellies, mustards, chutneys, and flavored vinegars

JAR	SIZE & STYLE	SUGGESTED USES FOR PRESERVING, SERVING & RECIPES
	Jelly jar/4 oz regular mouth	Jams, jellies, mustards, ketchups, dipping sauces, and small portion sizes
	Elite Collection, half pint size/8 oz wide mouth	Flavored mustards, chutneys, dressings, jellies, and jams; elegant enough to take from kitchen to table

These multiple sizes and shapes of jars aren't just good for various sizes of foods to be preserved, but they also present some fun opportunities for craft projects. So grab your favorite Mason jar and let's get crafting!

SAFETY WARNING: Since Mason jars are made of glass and will break and shatter if dropped or handled roughly, adult supervision is highly recommended with all craft projects in this book.

Mason Jar Summer Camp

Crafts with Jars

Mason jars, in all their various sizes and shapes, are a perfect canvas for your creativity—both inside and out. You can paint them and plant in them and use them to store your most precious memories. So pull out the glue, paint, and scissors, and let's get started on your very own Mason jar masterpiece. The possibilities are only limited to your imagination!

Summer Vacation Memory Jar

Don't you wish summer vacation could last forever? That you could ride your bike, play with friends, go to the beach, and travel with your family forever? Unfortunately, the first day of school arrives all too quickly. But with this fun project, you can easily bottle up your favorite summer memories and enjoy them all year long!

SUPPLIES

- Large Mason jar (quart size/32 oz.)
- Blue acrylic craft paint in flat finish
- Painter's tape (shape tape optional)
- Vacation pictures
- Photo paper
- Wooden skewers
- Shells, sand, and other mementos from vacation
- Paintbrush
- Scissors

INSTRUCTIONS

1 Create a water effect on the bottom of your Mason jar using painter's tape. You can use "shape tape" that can be found at a home improvement store or create your own wave detail look by cutting shapes out of straightedge painter's tape. Use your fingers to seal edges tightly.

2 Paint the bottom of the jar with blue acrylic craft paint.

3 Remove tape immediately. Let dry.

4 Choose vacation pictures you want to share in the jar. Print out the pictures onto photo printer paper.

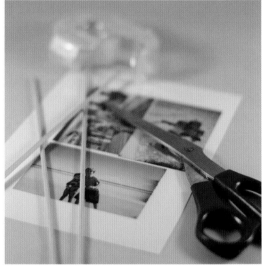

5 Cut out pictures and affix to wood skewers with tape.

6   Fill the jar with sand from vacation.
Arrange shells and/or other
mementos in bottom of jar.

7   Push pictures with the wooden
skewers into the sand.

Stained Glass Jar

Making stained glass with tissue paper and glue is a time-honored craft tradition that dates back long before even your parents were born. Seriously. And *that* is a very, very long time ago! Go crazy with this project and experiment with different sizes, colors, and shapes of tissue paper. Then light up your jar at night with a flameless candle and stand back to admire your stained glass handiwork.

SUPPLIES

- Mason jar (pint size/16 oz.)
- Tissue paper in a variety of colors
- Scissors
- Glue (school glue or decoupage medium)
- Water (if using school glue)
- Paintbrush

INSTRUCTIONS

1 Cut pieces of tissue paper into desired shapes.

2 Brush decoupage medium onto the outside of the jar. Or, if using school glue, thin it first by adding water (add 1 tablespoon of water for every 2 tablespoons of glue used). Use a thin layer, starting at the bottom and working in small areas.

3 Affix tissue paper to jar, overlapping slightly. Lightly brush the edges of the tissue paper with more glue or decoupage medium.

4 Use your brush and/or fingers to smooth down the tissue paper edges. Be careful not to tear.

5 Let dry overnight.

Sea Glass Mason Jars

Sea glass is a piece of history. Sure, it may have started out as a soda bottle or a glass or a vase that ended up in the ocean as trash or even in a shipwreck. But over decades it's been tossed and turned in the sand and surf, becoming smooth and tumbled and getting a frosty appearance. At one time, it was common to find pieces of sea glass along the shoreline. But a decline in glass bottle production and the popularity of recycling has made it harder and harder to find. With this project, you can create your own rare sea glass look with some glue and food coloring.

SUPPLIES

- Glue
- Food coloring in various colors
- Mason jars (pint size/16 oz.)
- Plastic cups or bowls
- Paintbrush
- Gloves

Quick Tip
For a different look, try painting the insides of the jars instead.

INSTRUCTIONS

1. Put on gloves. Add one to two drops of food coloring to the glue. Mix well.

2 Paint the outsides of the jars using a paintbrush. Use a light coat of paint.

3 Let dry overnight. The glue and food coloring mixture will be a bit runny. When drying, alternate between turning the jar upside down and right side up.

Note: This is not permanent dye so do not submerge in water.

SEA GLASS FACTS

Did You Know?

- Sea glass has been around for as long as man has made glass—which dates back 3,500 years ago.

- The most common colors of sea glass are kelly green, brown, and white (clear). Purple, blues in teals and turquoise, pinks, reds, and black are much harder to find.

- Sea glass is also called "Mermaid Tears." Folklore claimed that the frosted glass pieces that washed up on shore were the tears shed by mermaids when a sailor drowned at sea.

Painted & Distressed Mason Jars

There's really no right or wrong way to paint and distress a Mason jar. Pick a color, brush it on, and then use sandpaper to remove some paint to give it an aged look. That's what *distressed* means: taking something new and making it look old and antique.

SUPPLIES

- Acrylic craft paint in a flat finish
- Sandpaper (80 grit)
- Mason jars (pint size/16 oz.)
- Paintbrushes
- Clear coat spray sealer

Quick Tip

Before painting, wash the jars with warm, soapy water and wipe down with a cotton ball soaked in rubbing alcohol to help the paint stick. Let dry completely before painting.

INSTRUCTIONS

1 Paint jars with acrylic craft paint. Let dry.

2

Apply a second coat of paint. For best results, let dry overnight before proceeding to step 3.

Painting tip: paint around the top rim of the jar first. Turn upside down and paint the bottom half.

3

Fold sandpaper into one square inch. Use it to lightly sand or remove paint from raised letters and areas on the jars—and also around the top and bottom of the jar.

4

Spray with a clear coat sealant. Jars can be wiped down but should not be submerged in water or put in the dishwasher. The paint treatment is not permanent.

Paint Drip Jars

Have your parents ever asked you to make a mess? On purpose? Probably not. More likely they've asked you to clean one up. Until now. That's what this project is all about. Making a mess. In a Mason jar. With paint.

SUPPLIES

- Acrylic craft paint
- Mason jars (pint size/16 oz.)
- Water
- Plastic cups
- Spoon

Quick Tip
To use this jar as a vase, first put a small plastic cup inside of the jar to hold the water.

INSTRUCTIONS

1 Thin the paint with a few drops of water so it can pour easily, but isn't too runny. Mix well with a spoon.

2 Pour the first color into a jar.

3 Tilt the jar and pour out some paint.

4 For the next layer of paint, pour into the jar from the top rim. Repeat with the remaining colors.

5 When finished, tilt the jar gently to one side and pour out as much paint as possible.

6 Turn the jar right-side up to dry. It may take up to one week for the paint to dry completely. Do not fill with water. The paint treatment is not permanent.

Mason Jar Planter

Do you have a green thumb? Do you know what a green thumb is? No, it's not a thumb painted green. It's actually a term used to describe someone who likes to garden and grow plants. With this Mason jar planter project, you can test out your green thumb skills on a small scale to see if you have what it takes help a plant thrive.

SUPPLIES

- Mason jar (pint size/16 oz.)
- Plant of your choice (*see quick tip* for recommendations)
- Small rocks
- Pebbles
- Moss
- Potting soil
- Spoon
- Gloves

Quick Tip

Succulents—often referred to as cactus plants—are easy to care for and perfect for a Mason jar planter. They don't need a lot of water and can endure extended periods of drought, relying on the stored water and nutrients in their leaves.

INSTRUCTIONS

1 Fill the jar with pebbles up to the 1/4 mark on the side of the jar. This pebble layer allows water to drain from the soil.

2 Add a layer of small rocks to the jar, on top of the pebbles. This layer also helps with drainage.

3 Soak moss in water for a few seconds, then squeeze out any excess water. Place the moss on top of rocks. This creates an additional barrier so the soil doesn't fall into the pebbles and stones.

4 Put on gloves. Add potting soil.

5 Use your fingers to create a hole in the potting soil and insert your plant.

6 Add more potting soil to the jar to secure the plant. Water.

Mason Jar Merriment

Holiday Crafts with Jars

There's a Mason jar craft idea for every reason—and every season. Whether you're looking to scare up some Halloween treats or are dreaming of a white Christmas, these holiday crafts with Mason jars are sure to get you in the spirit by adding a touch of merriment to any holiday celebration.

Spring Jars: The Bunny, the Lamb & the Chick

Usher in spring with a *baa* and a *cheep* and a hippity hop with these cute and colorful Mason jars! These springtime creations can help brighten up any windowsill or table centerpiece during the spring season—and they also make perfect gifts!

SUPPLIES

- White acrylic craft paint
- Yellow acrylic craft paint
- Pink acrylic craft paint
- Spray paint in white, yellow, and pink
- Yellow feathers
- Felt pieces in white, yellow, and pink
- Cotton balls or white pompoms
- Black electrical tape
- 3 Mason jars (pint size/16 oz.)
- Wax paper
- Glue gun
- Contact glue (quick-dry multi-surface)
- Fabric glue
- Paintbrushes
- Scissors

Quick Tip
To minimize clean up, don't wash the brushes in between coats of paint. Simply store in sealable plastic bags until you're ready to use again!

INSTRUCTIONS

1 Paint the insides of the jars with white, yellow, and pink acrylic craft paint. Let dry. Paint a second coat.

2 Ask an adult to help spray paint the Mason jar bands with white, yellow, and pink spray paint. Let dry.

3 Cut felt pieces for ears, feathers, beak, and noses.

4 Use fabric glue to attach the white inserts on the pink bunny ears.

5 Use fabric glue to attach the pink inserts on the white lamb ears.

6 Use fabric glue to attach the yellow feathers to the yellow felt piece.

7 Screw spray painted lids on the jars. Use a glue gun to attach the ears to the bunny jar and the feathers to the duck jar.

8   Use a glue gun to attach the ears to the sides of the lamb jar and to also glue the pompoms (or cotton balls) to the Mason jar band.

9   Use contact glue to attach the eyes and noses.

10   On the bunny jar, cut strips of black electrical tape for whiskers.

Firecracker Rocket Jars

Shoot for the stars with these star spangled firecracker rocket jars. Used as a centerpiece or filled with treats, they're sure to make some noise at your next barbecue or picnic.

SUPPLIES

- White acrylic craft paint
- Blue acrylic craft paint
- Red acrylic craft paint
- Mason jars (wide mouth 1 ½ pint size/24 oz.)
- Star stickers
- Red, white, and blue colored tape
- Red, white, and blue cardstock paper
- Paintbrushes
- Tape
- Scissors
- Ruler

Quick Tip
Electrical tape is inexpensive and comes in a variety of colors. You can find it at the hardware store.

INSTRUCTIONS

1 Paint the insides of the jars with white, red, and blue acrylic craft paint. Let dry.

2 Use colored tape and stickers to decorate the jars.

3 Use colored paper or cardstock to create the rocket top. Place a bowl on top of the paper and trace around it. (Use a bowl approximately 6 ½ inches [16.5 cm] in diameter for a wide mouth mason jar top.)

4 Cut out the circle.

5 Use a ruler to find the center of the circle. Cut a slit in the paper to the center.

6   Fold around.

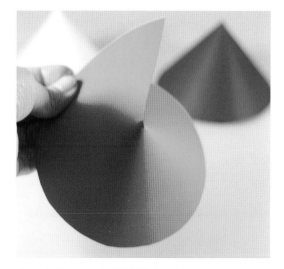

7   Staple to hold.

8   Use tape to attach the rocket top to the Mason jar.

Red, White & Blue Rice Votives

Shine a light on your patriotic pride with these all-American red, white, and blue Mason jar votives. Parade them out at your next Fourth of July celebration and let the flag waving begin!

SUPPLIES

- Long grain rice (6 cups/1 kg, uncooked)
- Food coloring in red and blue
- 2 Mason jars (quart size/32 oz.)
- 3 Mason jars (pint size/16 oz.)
- 2 cookie sheets
- Gloves
- Wax paper
- Water
- Tablespoon
- Tea light candles

Words of Caution

While food coloring is not dangerous or toxic—it's often used in many of the foods we eat and drink—it will stain skin, clothes, and surfaces. Take care to wear gloves before handling the food coloring, protect your surfaces with plastic, and wear a smock or old clothes.

INSTRUCTIONS

1 Measure out 2 cups (380 g) of uncooked long-grain rice each into two separate quart-size Mason jars (for a total of 4 cups [0.75 kg] of rice).

2 Add 4 tablespoons (2 oz.) of water to each jar. Screw on the lids and shake to mix.

3 Remove lids. Put on gloves and add 20 to 30 drops of blue food coloring to one jar and 20 to 30 drops of red food coloring to the second jar.

4 Screw on the lids and shake vigorously to mix up the color. Add more food coloring if a darker color is desired.

5 Cover cookie sheets with wax paper. Spread out the rice on the two cookie sheets to dry. Keep the blue and red rice on separate cookie sheets. Use a spatula to mix every 10 minutes. It will take 20 to 30 minutes for the rice to dry completely.

6 Layer the rice in jars using blue, plain white, and red.

7 Set a tea light in the middle of the rice. Ask an adult to light the candle.

Halloween Jars: Mummy, Pumpkin & Frankenstein

Scare up some serious tricks with these Halloween monster and pumpkin jars. Perfect for a costume party—or for stashing away your favorite Halloween treats.

SUPPLIES

- White acrylic craft paint
- Orange acrylic craft paint
- Green acrylic craft paint
- Orange spray paint
- White spray paint
- Green felt
- 3 Mason jars (pint size/16 oz.)
- Wine cork
- Green pipe cleaners
- 2 hardware nuts

- Duct tape or electrical tape
- Adhesive first-aid tape (½ inch/1 cm width)
- Wax paper
- Wiggle eyes
- Contact glue (quick-dry multi-surface) or glue gun
- Paintbrushes
- Knife

Quick Tip
The lids and bands can be painted with acrylic or latex paint and a brush, but they must first be painted with primer. Otherwise the paint will not adhere to the metal.

INSTRUCTIONS

1   Paint the insides of the jars with white, orange, and green acrylic craft paint. Let dry.

2   Spray paint one lid and band orange and one lid and band white. Let dry.

3   Glue lids to the bands.

4   With help of an adult, use a knife to cut 1/3 of the wine cork off.

5   Glue the wine cork to the top of the orange lid.

6   Add green pipe cleaner to the stem.

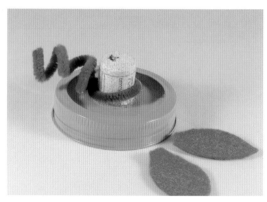

7   Cut leaf shapes from green felt and glue to the lid.

8 Glue hardware nuts to the sides of the green Frankenstein jar. Let dry.

9 Cut two 10-inch (25 cm) lengths of electrical tape and attach to the wax paper. Cut out various shapes for the eyes and mouth of the pumpkin jar, and the hair and mouth for the Frankenstein jar.

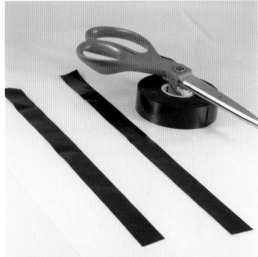

10 Peel off the wax paper from the back of the electrical tape eyes and mouth and attach to the pumpkin jar. Screw on the orange lid.

11 Peel off the wax paper from the back of the electrical tape Frankenstein hair and mouth. Attach to the jar. Glue on wiggle eyes. Screw on silver lid.

12 Attach the white lid to the mummy jar. Wrap the mummy jar with adhesive first-aid tape. Add wiggle eyes.

Turkey Jar Centerpiece

Feathers, felt, and some wiggly eyes transform a Mason jar into the perfect centerpiece for your family's Thanksgiving feast. You family will gobble it up!

SUPPLIES

- Brown acrylic craft paint
- Feathers
- Wiggle eyes
- Orange felt
- Red tape or felt
- Mason jar (pint size/16 oz.)
- Contact glue (quick-dry multi-surface)
- Glue gun
- Paintbrush

INSTRUCTIONS

1   Paint the inside of the jar with brown acrylic craft paint. Let dry. Apply a second coat of paint. Let dry.

2 Cut a teardrop shape from red electrical tape (or felt) and attach to the jar.

3 Cut a triangle shape from orange felt for the beak. Attach to the jar with contact glue. Let dry.

4 Attach the wiggle eyes with contact glue. Let dry.

4 Use a glue gun to attach the feathers to the inside of the top rim of the jar.

Car in a Mason Jar Snow Globe

Your favorite toy car takes center stage this holiday season with this easy, liquid-free car in a jar snow globe. This project is so easy to create, you'll want to make one for each and every one of your cars!

SUPPLIES

- Toy car
- Bottle brush tree
- Epsom salt
- Baker's twine or string
- Red jingle bells

- Mason jar (Elite Collection wide mouth pint sized/16 oz.)
- Tablespoon
- Scissors

INSTRUCTIONS

1. Remove the bottom from the bottle brush tree. It should easily screw off. Bend excess wire at the end of the tree (you could also ask your parents to cut with a wire cutter).

2 Use baker's twine or string to tie the tree to the top of the car. Either string through the windows or wrap around the entire car.

3 Add 4 to 6 tablespoons of Epsom salt to the bottom of the Mason jar.

4 Add the car and screw on the top. Ask an adult to help wrap the Mason jar band with baker's twine (or string) and add jingle bells.

Santa Suit Jar

Add a little ho, ho, ho to your holidays with this Santa suit Mason jar. Decked out with a felt belt and buckle, it will look perfect sitting on a mantel with care . . . waiting for St. Nicholas, who's soon to be there!

SUPPLIES

- Red acrylic craft paint
- Black felt
- Yellow felt
- Mason jar (wide mouth pint size/16 oz.)
- Glue (quick-dry) or glue gun
- Paintbrush

INSTRUCTIONS

1   Paint the inside of the jar with red acrylic craft paint. Let dry. Apply a second coat of red paint. Let dry.

2 Cut a length of black felt 10 ½ inches (26 cm) long by 2 inches (5 cm) wide. This will be Santa's belt.

3 Cut a 2 ½-inch (6.25 cm) square of yellow felt. Cut out a center square that is 1 ½ inches (3.75 cm). This will be Santa's belt buckle.

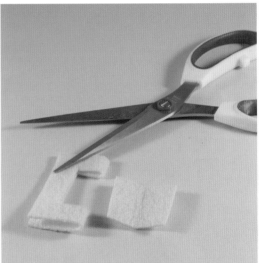

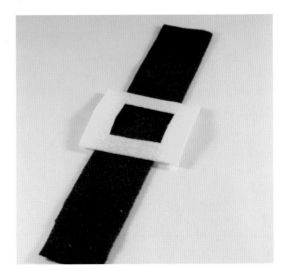

4

Use the quick dry glue or a glue gun to attach the black felt belt around the center of the Mason jar. Glue where the ends meet up.

5

Center the yellow felt square buckle on the black belt. Use contact glue to attach the felt to the jar.

Managing the Mayhem

Mason Jar Storage Ideas

Cleaning up your mess is a welcome chore with these stylish, mess-managing, out-of-the-toy-box Mason jar storage ideas. Personalize them to suit your style and taste. There are plenty of Mason jar sizes and shapes to wrangle just about any toy, craft supply, or favorite collection!

Glitter & Glam Jars

Your art supplies will sparkle and shine with these painted and glittered Mason jars storage cups.

SUPPLIES

- Pink acrylic craft paint
- Blue acrylic craft paint
- Pink glitter
- Blue glitter
- Glue
- Pink & blue sticker embellishments (optional)
- Painter's tape
- Mason jars (pint size/16 oz.)
- Paintbrushes
- Foam brushes
- Scissors

Quick Tip

Remove painter's tape immediately after the paint is applied. If you wait until it dries you may take the paint off with the tape.

INSTRUCTIONS

1 Tape off the bottom half of the jars. Use your fingers to seal the edges.

2 Paint the jars with pink and blue acrylic craft paint. Remove the tape immediately. Let dry.

3 Tape off the jars again and apply glue with the foam brush. Cover the painted area. Take care not to pull up the paint.

4 Sprinkle generously with glitter. Remove the tape and let dry.

Optional
Apply embellishment
stickers to the jars.

Pig-Topped Piggy Bank Mason Jar

A pink painted pig sitting atop a Mason jar is a new twist on the piggy bank. An added plus: with the glass jar you can easily watch as your dollars and cents add up.

SUPPLIES

- Plastic pig figurine
- Pink spray paint
- Mason jar (pint size/16 oz.)
- Contact glue (quick-dry multi-surface)
- Gloves

Quick Tip

Inexpensive small plastic animals can be found at most large craft stores or in the party favor section of party supply stores.

INSTRUCTIONS

1 Put on the gloves.

2 Glue the Mason jar lid to the band by applying a thin layer of glue along the rim of the band. Press the lid on top into the glue. Let dry.

3 Glue the plastic pig to top of the lid. Let dry.

3 With an adult's help, spray paint the lid with the pig glued on with pink spray paint. Let dry. (If you don't want to use spray paint, you can use regular paint. You first need to use a primer on the lid and pig or the paint won't stick.)

Safety First
Use contact glue and spray paint in well-ventilated areas.

Mini Fig LEGO-Topped Jars

You'll never hear "clean up your LEGOs" again with these mini fig LEGO-topped storage jars. Sort by color, shape, or even LEGO kits, so finding the perfect piece to build your next masterpiece is just a jar away!

SUPPLIES

- Blue, red, and yellow spray paint
- Mason jars (pint size/16 oz.)
- Mounting putty (or glue, *see quick tip*)
- LEGO bricks
- Mini Fig LEGO characters

Quick Tip
Mounting putty is a non-permanent way to attach LEGO people to the tops of the jars; this way, you can still play with your favorite LEGO people when they are not keeping guard over the LEGO pieces.

INSTRUCTIONS

1 With an adult's help, spray paint the Mason jar lids and bands in blue, red, and yellow.

2 Once completely dry, glue the bands to the lids. Apply glue along the inside rim of the lid. Then press the band firmly in place. Let dry completely.

3 Separate the LEGO pieces by color into the jars.

4 Attach the mini fig LEGO character on top using mounting putty.

Sporty Storage Jars

Keep your ticket stubs, ribbons, and medals stored in style with these ball-topped Mason jars. You can even show you team pride by spray painting the Mason jar lids and bands with your favorite baseball, basketball, and soccer team colors.

SUPPLIES

- 3 wooden knobs
- Mason jars (pint size/16 oz.)
- White acrylic craft paint
- Orange acrylic craft paint
- Silver spray paint
- Fine-tipped markers in black and red
- Paintbrushes or foam brushes
- Contact glue (quick-dry multi-surface)
- Pencil

Quick Tip
Use an old egg carton as a mess-free way to paint the knobs.

INSTRUCTIONS

1 Paint the wooden knobs with white and orange paint. Paint two knobs white (one for a baseball and one for a soccer ball) and one orange (for a basketball). Let dry. Paint a second coat. Let dry.

2 With an adult's help, spray paint the lids and bands silver.

3 Use a pencil to draw lines for the basketball on the orange knob and for the baseball and soccer ball on white knobs.

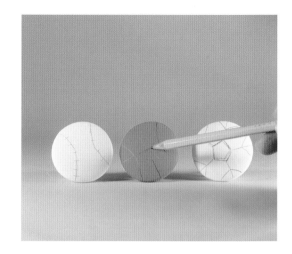

4 Fill in with fine-point black and red markers. Let dry.

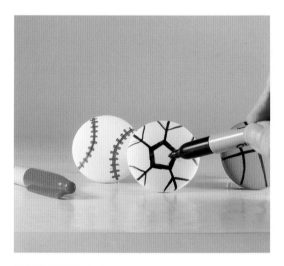

5 Use contact glue to attach the lids to the bands. Let dry.

6 Use contact glue to attach the knobs to the tops of the Mason jar lids. Let dry.

Chalkboard Label Storage Jars

Who wants to hide away crayons and pencils in boxes and drawers when you can make such a vibrant, colorful display of your art supplies on your desk with large Mason jars? Chalkboard paint is a fun and easy way to add labels to your jars.

SUPPLIES

- Chalkboard paint
- Painter's tape
- 2 Mason jars (1 liter/34 oz. and 1.5 liter/1.6 quart)*
- Chalk
- Foam brush
- Decoupage medium (optional)

*These are specialty jars made from an Italian manufacturer and sold in US at major retailers including Target, Container Store, Carsons, and at Amazon.com.

Quick Tip

For a clean edge on the chalkboard paint label, brush a thin layer of decoupage medium along the edge of the painter's tape and let dry completely before applying paint.

INSTRUCTIONS

1 Make sure the jar's surface is clean and dry. Wash with warm soapy water and wipe with rubbing alcohol on cotton balls.

2 Use painter's tape to tape off the area for the chalkboard label.

3 Paint taped off area with chalkboard paint using a foam brush. Let dry.

4 Apply a second or third coat, as needed. Let dry between coats of paint. Remove painter's tape. Let dry overnight.

5 Season the chalkboard label by rubbing over the area with the side of the chalk. Wipe away with a chalkboard eraser or paper towel.

6 Fill with craft supplies and label the jar's contents with chalk.

Sharing the Mason Jar Love

Gift Ideas

They say it's better to give than to receive, which is especially true for the person on the receiving end of these creative Mason jar gift ideas! From a mustache mug for Father's Day to a pencil holder for your teacher, you'll have the best time creating custom, homemade gifts for the favorite people in your life.

Mustache Mug for Dad

Your dad doesn't have to sport a real mustache to enjoy his morning cup of joe in this fun-loving mustache mug. The best part: he'll think of you with each and every mustachioed sip.

SUPPLIES

- Mason jar mug (pint size/16 oz.)
- Glass paint in black
- Wax paper (or contact paper)
- Painter's tape
- Pencil
- Scissors
- Paintbrush

Quick Tip

You can find free mustache printables online. Simply type in "free mustache printable" in a Google search. Then switch to Google Image view to see your options. Then just download, resize, and print out your chosen design.

INSTRUCTIONS

1 Make a mustache stencil.

   a. Print out a mustache image (*see quick tip*). Place wax paper (or contact paper) over the image and trace with a pencil.

b. Place painter's tape over the traced image on the wax paper.

c. Mark the center, fold in half, and cut out the center of the image.

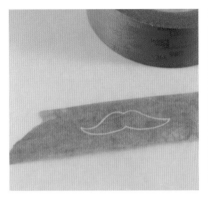 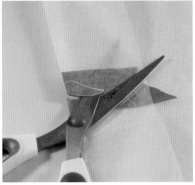 

2 Affix the stencil to the mug. Use your finger to seal tightly along the edges.

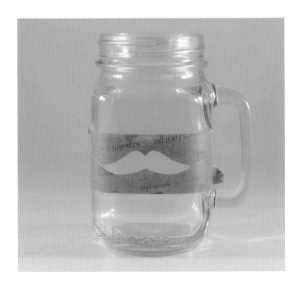

3 Apply black glass paint with a paintbrush.

4 Remove tape immediately.

5 Let air dry for 1 hour.

6 To set paint to make the mug safe for washing, place on a cookie sheet or in a baking pan in a cool oven. Heat to 350°F (175°C). Bake 30 minutes. Turn off the oven and let cool in the oven. Remove. Hand washing is recommended, though manufacturers state that the mug will be top rack dishwasher safe.

Lips Mug for Mom

Pucker up and give your mom a big, permanent kiss with this adorable lips mug.

SUPPLIES

- Mason jar mug (pint size/16 oz.)
- Pink glass paint
- Wax paper (or contact paper)
- Painter's tape
- Pencil
- Scissors
- Paintbrush

Quick Tip

You can find free lips printables online. Simply type in "free lip printable" in a Google search. Then switch to Google Image view to see your options. Download, resize, and print out.

INSTRUCTIONS

1 Make a lips stencil.

a. Print out the lips image. Place wax paper (or contact paper) over the image and trace with a pencil.

b. Place painter's tape over the traced image on the wax paper.

c. Mark the center, fold in half, and cut out the center of the image.

 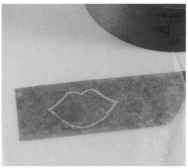 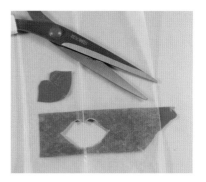

2 Affix the stencil to the mug. Use your finger to seal tightly along the edges.

3 Apply pink glass paint with a paintbrush.

4 Remove tape immediately.

5 Let air dry for 1 hour.

6 To set paint to make the mug safe for washing, place on a cookie sheet or in a baking pan in a cool oven. Heat to 350°F (175°C). Bake 30 minutes. Turn off the oven and let cool in the oven. Remove. Hand washing is recommended, though manufacturers state that the mug will be top rack dishwasher safe.

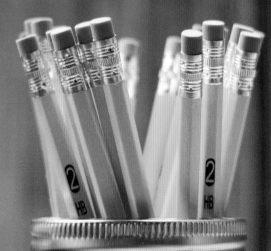

School Days Jars for Teacher

Thank your teacher for helping you learn those ABCs and 123s with these clever No. 2 pencil and chalkboard Mason jars. A perfect gift to hold pencils and pens, rulers, chalk . . . and more.

SUPPLIES

- Chalkboard paint
- Yellow acrylic craft paint
- Number and letter stickers
- Mason jars (pint size/ 16 oz.)
- Sandpaper
- Chalk
- Clear coat spray sealant
- Paintbrush

Quick Tip

If you don't want to invest in a jar of chalkboard paint, you can easily make your own in any color you desire. Simply mix together ½ cup acrylic or latex paint with 1 ½ teaspoon un-sanded grout.

INSTRUCTIONS

1 Paint the jars with yellow acrylic craft paint and chalkboard paint. Start by painting around the top of the jar. Flip over and paint the bottom. Let dry. Apply a second coat of paint. Let dry.

To minimize clean up, don't wash brushes in between coats of paint. Simply store in sealable plastic bags.

2   Use sandpaper to distress the jars lightly. Concentrate on the raised areas around the jar.

3   Apply stickers to the pencil jar.

Season the chalkboard jar with chalk. Rub chalk over the jar using the side of the chalk. Wipe off with a towel or chalkboard eraser.

5

Seal the yellow pencil jar with a clear coat spray sealant.

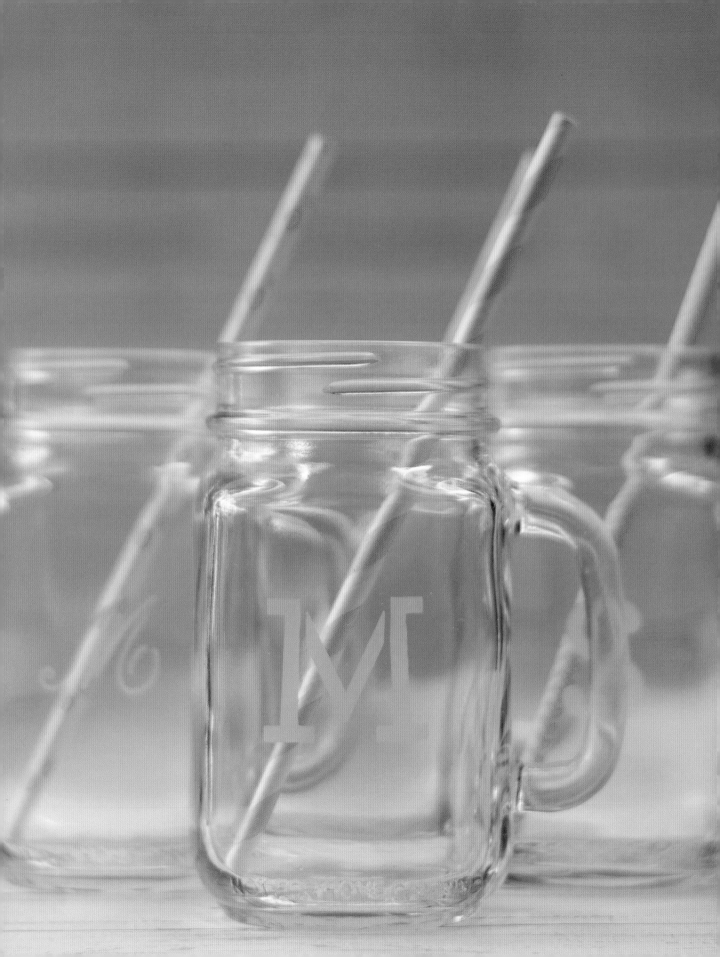

Monogram Mason Jar Mugs for the Family

Make your mark on a mug with this etched glass Mason jar project. A great gift idea for Mom, Dad, and your siblings. This way, there's no confusion about whose glass is whose!

SUPPLIES

- Mason jar mug (pint size/16 oz.)
- Stencils
- Etching medium
- Paintbrush*
- Gloves

depending on the brand of etching medium used, a brush may be included

Quick Tip

Adhesive monogram stickers are easy to work with, especially when using a glass or curved surface. You can find them at most craft stores, typically located near the paints and painting supplies.

INSTRUCTIONS

1 Clean the surface area with rubbing alcohol, soap, and water. Dry.

Safety First

Adult supervision is needed when using etching cream. It's recommended that you wear plastic gloves and an old shirt with long sleeves, and be sure to work in a well-ventilated area.

2 Attach a monogram stencil to the Mason jar.

3 Wear protective gloves to apply the etching medium (with adult supervision). Use a thick layer of etching medium in a generous, even coat.

3 Let the etching cream sit on the surface for 15 minutes. Wash off using warm soapy water. Remove the stencil.

Check the etching cream instructions to see if the mugs will be dishwasher safe.

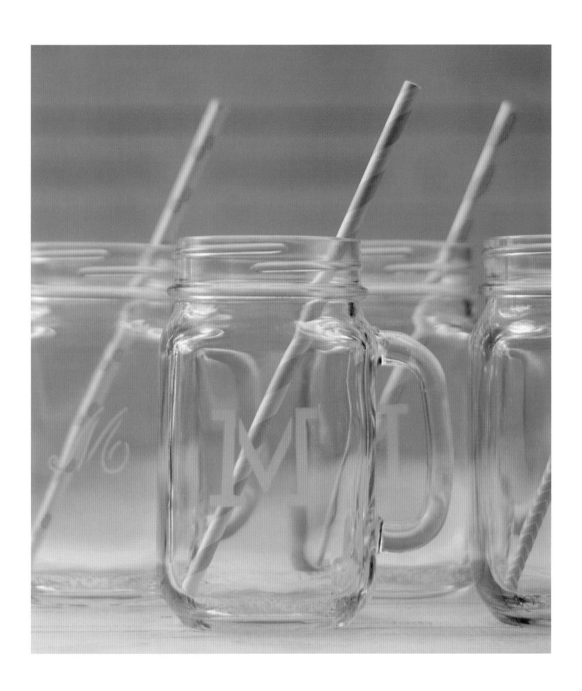

Picture Collage for Grandma & Grandpa

Whether your grandparents live around the corner or across the country, they'll love this picture collage vase celebrating all the special moments in your life.

SUPPLIES

- Mason jar (quart size/ 32 oz.)
- Photos for scanning
- Copy paper
- Decoupage medium
- Foam brush
- Scissors

Quick Tip

You can edit the pictures before printing to lighten up the exposure and sharpen the images using free photo editing software online. Just Google "free online photo editing" for options to explore.

INSTRUCTIONS

1 Scan photos and print out on copier paper. Let dry overnight.

2 Cut out the photos.

3 Apply the decoupage medium to the jar.

4 Attach a picture and use the decoupage medium to cover the edges. Brush the decoupage medium over the entire photo.

5 Keep applying the medium and pictures, overlapping them slightly. Use medium and/or your fingers to smooth down the edges.

6 Once the surface is completely covered with photographs, give the jar one final coat of decoupage medium. Let dry.

Thumbprint Sunflower Jar

Finger painting isn't just for paper anymore. Brighten up a painted Mason jar vase with a personalize thumbprint flower—made just by you. And since no two fingerprints are alike, your thumbprint vase will be one of a kind!

SUPPLIES

- White acrylic craft paint
- Yellow acrylic craft paint
- Brown acrylic craft paint
- Green acrylic craft paint
- Mason jar (pint size/ 16 oz.)
- Paintbrush
- Sandpaper

INSTRUCTIONS

1 Paint the Mason jar with white acrylic craft paint. Let dry. Apply a second coat of white acrylic craft paint. Let dry overnight for best results.

2 Use a small square of sandpaper to remove some paint from around the top rim and on the raised print of the Mason jar. Wipe clean with a paper towel.

3 Dip either your pointer finger or thumb in brown paint. Push your finger with paint on it onto the center of the jar. Wash your hands.

4 Dip either your pointer finger or thumb in yellow paint. Push your finger with paint on it onto the jar around the brown center to make a flower petal. Dip your finger in yellow paint again and repeat around the brown center. Wash your hands. Let the jar dry.

5 Once the paint is dry, use a fine-tipped paintbrush to make seeds in the center of the flower with green paint. Let dry.

Colorful Candied Popcorn in Mason Jars

Add a pop of color to boring old white popcorn with this colorful candied popcorn recipe . . . and when you pop it into your mouth, you'll get a mix of sweet and salty flavor.

SUPPLIES

- 1 cup (200 g) sugar
- ½ teaspoon (2.5 g) salt
- ¼ cup (2 oz.) water
- 1 teaspoon (5 g) vanilla
- Food coloring
- 6 cups (1.2 kg) popped popcorn
- 4 medium bowls
- 4 small bowls
- Wax paper
- Spoons
- Mason jars (any size)

INSTRUCTIONS

1 Divide the popcorn evenly into four separate containers.

Safety First
Adult supervision and help is a must for this project since boiling liquid on the stove is involved.

2 Have an adult boil the sugar, salt, and water in a small saucepan. Stir constantly and boil until you can't stir down the bubbles.

3 Remove from the heat and add 1 teaspoon of vanilla.

4 Divide the mixture evenly into four small bowls. Add 1 to 2 drops of food coloring and mix well.

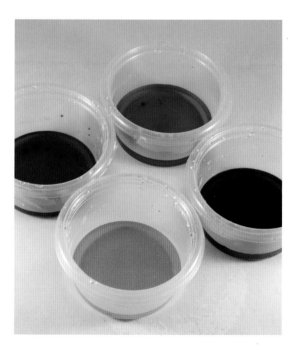

5   Pour one of each color over a container of popcorn. Mix well.

6   Spread out the popcorn on wax paper to dry.

7   Once dry, mix colorful candied popcorn together. Store in Mason jars.

Mad Science with Mason Jars

Jarring Science Experiments

Put on your lab coat and goggles and get ready to make a fun mess! In fact, as you roll up your sleeves and get your hands in on the mess-making action, you won't realize that you're learning a thing or two about science along the way. But before you grab the food coloring, measuring cups, glue, and flour, you first need to promise Mom and Dad that you'll help with the clean up!

Color Change Flowers

Want a blue flower? Or green? Or yellow? Just change it with food coloring. You can easily turn a white flower just about any color you want in just 24 hours. And if you let the flower sit in the colored water for longer, the color just gets deeper and darker. This fun experiment shows exactly how a flower drinks by drawing water up its stem and up into the petals.

SUPPLIES

- 4 Mason jars (pint size/16 oz.)
- Food coloring in assorted colors
- White carnations
- Water
- Scissors

Quick Tip
Use the markings on the side of the Mason jar to find the one-cup fill line. No measuring cups needed!

INSTRUCTIONS

1 Fill the Mason jars with one cup of cold water.

2 Add 20 to 30 drops of food coloring to the water.

3 Cut the flower stems on a diagonal.

4 Place one freshly cut flower in each Mason jar with colored water.

5 Check back every few hours to see how the flowers are progressing. It could take from 24 hours to a few days for the flowers to soak up the colored water.

Bubbling Brew

You'll definitely feel like a mad scientist as you concoct this colorful, bubbling brew. Stand back and watch as the chemical reaction between an acid (like vinegar) and a base (like baking soda) explodes in a volcano of colorful bubbles!

INGREDIENTS & SUPPLIES

- Baking soda
- Distilled white vinegar
- Dish soap
- Vinegar
- Food coloring

- 4 Mason jars (4 ounce jelly jars)
- Measuring cup
- Measuring spoon
- Plastic spoons
- Deep dish pan

INSTRUCTIONS

1 Fill four mason jars ¼ of the way up with vinegar. Place in a deep-dish pan (this experiment gets messy!).

2 Mix in food coloring.

3 Add a squirt of dish soap.

4 Scoop out a heaping spoon of baking soda.

5 Add baking soda to the Mason jars..

6 Watch as your colorful brew bubbles up.

Ooey Gooey Slime

Science can be fun when you're creating something ooey and gooey and slippery and slimy! With this easy-to-follow recipe, you'll learn firsthand about the properties of polymers as you mix and stretch and pull apart—and, best of all, play with—your homemade slime.

INGREDIENTS & SUPPLIES

- 8-oz bottle of white glue
- 1 teaspoon (5 g) Borax
- Large mixing bowl (or disposable plastic container)
- Spoon
- Measuring cup
- Measuring spoons
- Food coloring
- Water
- Mason jar (wide mouth pint size/ 16 oz.)

Quick Tip
Borax can be found in most grocery stores in the laundry detergent aisle. It has many uses and can be found as an ingredient in some laundry detergents and toothpaste brands. It also can be used to clean kitchens and bathrooms, to get rid of bugs, and to preserve fresh flowers.

INSTRUCTIONS

1 Empty the entire bottle of glue into a mixing bowl (or disposable plastic container for easier clean-up).

2 Fill the empty glue bottle with warm water, put the cap on, and shake. Pour into the mixing bowl. Mix well until the glue and water are combined.

3 Add food coloring to the glue and water mixture. Start with one or two drops and mix well. Add more food coloring if you want more color.

4 Fill a measuring cup with ½ cup (4 oz) of warm water. Add 1 teaspoon (5 g) of Borax and mix well.

5 Slowly add a little of the Borax solution to the food coloring, glue, and water mixture and stir. You'll immediately start to see how the molecules change as the substance gets sticky and harder to stir.

6 Use your hands to continue stirring the solution.

7 When you're finished playing, store in a tightly sealed Mason jar.

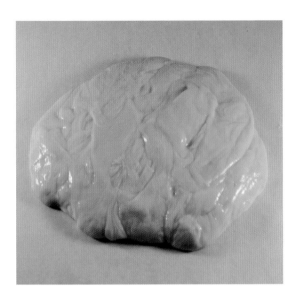

Homemade Play-Dough

It's almost impossible not to taste play-dough, right? There's just something about it—the colors, the texture, the smell, the name—that beckons you to take a bite! And while I don't recommend you eat this homemade play-dough, it is made from common non-toxic ingredients that can be found in the kitchen.

INGREDIENTS & SUPPLIES

- ½ cup (100 g) flour
- ¼ cup (50 g) salt
- 1 teaspoon (5 g) cream of tartar (can be found in spice section of super-market)
- 1 teaspoon (5 g) cooking oil
- ¼ cup boiling water

- 1 tablespoon flavored, colored gelatin dessert mix
- 4 Mason jars (wide mouth pint size/16 oz.)
- Measuring cup
- Measuring spoons
- Bowl
- Mixing spoon

Quick Tip

You can substitute flavored drink mixes for the gelatin. And if you want a more vibrant color, add a few drops of food coloring.

INSTRUCTIONS

1. Mix the flour, salt, cream of tartar, and oil in a bowl. Stir.

2. Boil water in a kettle. Have an adult pour the boiling water into a measuring cup to the ¼ cup mark.

3 Add 1 tablespoon of flavored, colored gelatin to the boiling water. Stir until dissolved.

4 Pour boiling water and gelatin mixture into the bowl of dry ingredients. Mix well.

5 Let sit for 5 minutes to cool.

A WORD OF WARNING

If you are tempted to take a taste, it's salty. Very, very salty. So have a big glass of water ready!

6 Work with your hands until smooth. Add flour (a little at a time) if the mixture is too sticky.

7 Store in Mason jars and refrigerate. With frequent use, play-dough can last for a few weeks.

Color Burst in a Jar

Did you know that not all liquids are the same? Some liquids are heavier—called denser, in science terms—than others. Put this to the test with water, oil, and food coloring. You might just be surprised to learn which liquids are heavier (denser) than others.

INGREDIENTS & SUPPLIES

- Food coloring (red, blue, yellow)
- Vegetable oil
- Mason jar (wide mouth quart size/32 oz.)
- Measuring spoon
- Measuring cup or small bowl
- Spoon

INSTRUCTIONS

1 Fill the jar with warm water.

2 In a measuring cup (or small bowl) measure out 3 tablespoons vegetable oil.

3 Add 3 to 4 drops of red, blue, and yellow food coloring.

4 Mix with a spoon.

5 Pour the oil and food coloring mixture into the Mason jar.

6 Watch as the food coloring explodes!

Were you surprised to discover that oil is less dense than water and that's why it floated to the top? And that the food coloring is heavier than the oil, and that's why it didn't dissolve in the oil, but instead sank and dissolved in the water below?

Layered Kid Cocktail

This is one part science and two parts delicious. I mean, seriously, what's more fun than an easy experiment that results in a great looking—and tasting—concoction? Not to mention clean-up is as easy as drinking the finished project!

INGREDIENTS & SUPPLIES

- Three different colored beverages with different sugar content (look for at least 10 to 15 grams difference between each one)
- Mason jar (pint size)
- Ice

INSTRUCTIONS

1 Fill the Mason jar to the top with ice.

2 Pour the beverage with the highest sugar content into the jar until it fills 1/3 of the jar.

3 Very slowly pour in the beverage with the second greatest sugar content. Pour directly onto an ice cube to slow it down.

4 Very slowly, pour the least sugary beverage on top.

5 Add a straw and enjoy!

Here's the secret to the science: sugar content. The drink with the greatest grams of sugar is denser, and that's why it goes on the bottom. You can then keep layering with drinks that have less sugar than the one below.

Acknowledgments

First and foremost, I would like to acknowledge and thank my family—my husband, Mike, and my children, Sam and Molly—for their infinite patience and understanding as I painted, glued, and photographed countless Mason jars in the making of this book. I could not have done it all without their unending support and love.

I would also like to thank Julie Matysik at Sky Pony Press who plucked me out of blog land obscurity and entrusted this very creative book idea in my amateur hands. Her encouragement and infectious enthusiasm for this project kept me going, especially during those days when the Mason jar craft vision in my head did not quite translate to the jar in my hand.

Finally, I would be remiss if I didn't give a shout out to the very talented KariAnne at Thistlewood Farms blog. She is the mastermind who suggested I start a blog devoted exclusively to Mason jar craft projects. Which turned out to be the very same blog that brought Sky Pony Press knocking at my door.

About the Author

Linda Braden may be a Mason jar enthusiast, but she's new to the world of Mason jars. She can't share fond memories of canning alongside multiple generations of women in her family. She didn't grow up with a basement brimming with Mason jars. In fact, her childhood home didn't even *have* a basement. And while she may have missed out on the joys of Mason jars during her formative years, she's making up for that now—forging new memories with her children and a newfound community of Mason jar lovers she's successfully cultivated online.

But instead of using Mason jars for their intended purpose—canning and preserving fresh foods—Linda's focus is on unconventional uses with Mason jars of all shapes and sizes. She paints them. She glues things to them. She fills them with fake snow, bottle brush trees, and toy cars. She wraps them with wire, adorns them with grocery store flowers, and hangs them from her windows. She is forever looking for new and unique ways to incorporate Mason jars into her home décor, holidays, gifts, and parties. And she shares her Mason jar projects and ideas, complete with detailed, easy-to-follow tutorials, on her Mason Jar Crafts Love blog (www.masonjarcraftslove.com).

Linda's interest in Mason jars first surfaced on her DIY and home décor blog, It All Started With Paint (www.itallstartedwithpaint.com). Her Mason jar projects took on a life of their own, sparking the idea for her blog devoted exclusively to Mason jar crafts.

Index

A

acrylic craft paint. (See paint)

adhesives

    colored tape, 37, 40, 53

    contact glue (quick-dry, multi-surface), 35, 37, 47, 53–54, 61, 63, 71–72, 76, 79, 81

    decoupage medium, 14, 83, 105–107

    duct tape, 47

    electrical tape, 35, 37, 39, 47, 49, 54

    fabric glue, 35–36

    first-aid tape, 47

    glue, 13–14, 17–18, 67–68

    mounting putty, 75–76

    painter's tape, 9, 67, 83–84, 89–90, 93

    tape, 39, 41

    white glue, 127

B

baker's twine, 57–58

baking soda, 123–124

bottle brush tree, 57

C

candle, 13, 43, 45

chalk, 83, 85, 97, 99

chalkboard paint. (See paint)

clear coat spray sealant, 97, 99

contact glue. (See adhesives)

cooking oil. (See oil)

copy paper. (See paper)

cork. (See wine cork)

cotton balls, 21, 35, 37, 83

craft paint. (See paint)

cream of tartar, 133

D

decoupage medium. (See adhesives)

dish soap, 123–124

duct tape. (See adhesives)

E

epsom salt, 57–58

etching medium, 101–102

F

fabric glue. (See adhesives)

feathers, 35–36, 53, 55

felt, 35–36, 47–48, 53–54, 61–63

flour, 133, 135

foam brush, 37–38, 79, 83–84, 105

food coloring, 17–18, 43–44, 113–114, 119–120, 123–125, 127–129, 133, 137–139

G

gelatin dessert mix, 133–134

gift ideas

    all occasions, 35, 97, 101, 105, 109, 113

    Father's day, 89

    Mother's day, 93

    teacher, 97

glass paint. (See paint)

glitter, 67, 69